IMAGES
of England

CHESTERFIELD
A CENTURY OF CHANGE

IMAGES
of England

CHESTERFIELD
A CENTURY OF CHANGE

Roy Thompson

TEMPUS

A corner of the churchyard in 1952. Early evening judging by the shadows, and the old gentlemen could be waiting for the adjacent Crooked Spire Inn to open its doors. The scene has changed since then. The Vicarage, on the other side of Church Way, disappeared in the 1980s to make way for a new development, the highway now has bus stands and much traffic, the Inn has now become the trendy Slug and Fiddle. Thankfully the churchyard remains much the same.

Frontispiece: The banks of the River Hipper near the 'Dog Kennels', *c.* 1901.

First published 2002

Tempus Publishing Limited
The Mill, Brimscombe Port,
Stroud, Gloucestershire, GL5 2QG

British Library Cataloguing in Publication Data.
A catalogue record for this book is available from the British Library.

ISBN 0 7524 2624 9

Typesetting and origination by Tempus Publishing Limited
Printed in Great Britain by Midway Colour Print, Wiltshire

Contents

Low Pavement at the start of the century and the horse-drawn tram has reversed its coach at the town terminus. The façade of the street, though slightly altered from this view, has been commendably preserved but little remains of what was behind it, and all the old yards on this section have been built over.

Introduction

'God made the Country but man made the Town'

To detail the various changes which took place in Chesterfield in the twentieth century is quite impossible in a couple of pages. What follows, then, are strokes from a very broad brush and somewhat subjective.

The twentieth century opened in Chesterfield with a long-reigning Queen on the throne, and closed with another Queen who had ruled for nearly half the century. In that time the town grew from a population of under 20,000 to over five times that number after borough boundaries had expanded to include neighbouring areas. Paradoxically, though maybe in part due to the expansion, the early years of the twentieth century show the start of a residential move out of the town which has gained in pace with the passage of time. This trend could be said to have started with the removal of the notorious 'Dog Kennels', an overcrowded slum area of more than 200 dwellings to the south of Low Pavement. The removal of these old, unsanitary houses became the personal campaign of the Mayor of 1910-1911, Charles Paxton Markham, who paid for the scheme himself. A grateful council responded by naming the new road after the benefactor.

Chesterfield stands on deposits of coal and clay and the winning and use of these had produced industries contributing significantly to the town's economy. Other industries joined these in the early century, feeding off them by supplying equipment, or using their production. Sheepbridge, the Markham Company, Plowrights, Bryan Donkin and the Tube Works, local giants all, thrived and expanded in this period, aided by increased demand in the 1914 war. By this time the town was surrounded by collieries like Markham, Ireland, Warsop, Arkwright, Grassmoor and many others. They and their support industries fed the local economy and provided employment for what was now an industrial, rather than a market, town. Indeed cast iron signs on trunk roads leading to the borough welcomed visitors to the 'Centre of Industrial England'.

Much manpower was lost when the 1939 war came and, where possible, women stood in for the labour called to the colours. National programmes of post-war rebuilding meant full employment for some years in most industries but major changes mid-century began to affect national and local ways of life for the foreseeable future. As new oil reserves were found, plastics began to take the place of steel and the production of iron slowed down, as did most of the industries which supported them. Many blast furnaces closed and with them the need for coke, and thus coal was reduced, making some old collieries uneconomic. And with the advent of North Sea gas the demand for coal fell even more, not helped by the Clean Air Act being adopted by local authorities, which forced consumers to use smokeless fuels. The pruning of the national rail network and the demise of the steam locomotives were further factors in the reduced demand for coal and this also signalled the end for two of the town's three railway stations, the Great Central (LNER) and the Market Place (LDEC), both going out of service in 1950s and 1960s.

Gradually, what could be termed the staple industries of the town lost profitability, shrank their labour forces and eventually closed. The Staveley furnaces, coke ovens and pipe plants, Bryan Donkin, Sheepbridge, the Avenue Coking plant, Plowrights and, eventually, the Markham Co., which had recently made segments for the London Underground and boring machines for the channel tunnel. Even Robinson & Sons, one of the town's largest employers for many years, had to reduce its work force in the face of demand, loss of some products and increased competition from multi-national companies.

All is not 'doom and gloom' on the industrial front, however. Although the deep coal mines have gone, open-cast mining continues on several sites, although it is now less labour intensive. Many small industries have become established in surrounding trading estates, turning out specialised high value products. Maybe in the 21st century one or more of these may become another Markhams or Sheepbridge.

The advent of supermarkets put many small shopkeepers out of business, reducing small convenience shopping to a minimum. But the growth in the number of car owners has resulted in more mini-supermarkets at petrol stations, restoring the balance somewhat.

Service industries have mushroomed in the area too, with building societies, some becoming new banks, proliferating in the town centre. Although the 1960s AGD building has gone, a new edifice has risen from its ashes. The town has become a popular shopping centre – indeed a tourist attraction – together with its ancient market and the proximity of a major motorway, the M1.

A fine new hospital has now served the town since the 1980s, and in the 1990s a whole section of the town was bieng renewed with the Vicar Lane development.

It is hoped that the images inside will remind readers of the town's past – not always as pleasant as one may remember it, but still worth recalling – and demonstrate that Chesterfield now, as ever, has much to admire.

Acknowledgements

Grateful thanks are due to everyone who helped with photographs, permission to reproduce them, assistance and information, in particular: Mr David Howes, Mr Alec Jackson, the staff of the Chesterfield Museum and the Local History Section of Chesterfield Library, Mr George Martin, Mr Ken Oldfield, Mr David Priestnall, Mr A.G. (Peter) Henson, Mr Peter J. Shelton and Mr David Roberts.

Special thanks go to my daughter, Helen, for her time and skill in typing the manuscript at short notice.

Thanks, of course, to my wife for her patience and encouragement.

One
Bits of the Old Town

All the houses at this end of Vicar Lane in 1923 were removed to erect St James' Hall, which served as a parish hall for St Mary's, and stood for about 100 years. On Lordsmill Street may be seen the Scarsdale Brewery offices and the Anchor Inn. The Victoria School on the extreme right of the photograph had lasted for ninety years before making way for a new bus station in 1934.

Beetwell Street in 1970 still had shops on the south side after the opposite row had been demolished, but they were soon to be removed for the new police headquarters.

The old courthouse in the 1970s. Magistrates had used this old building for Petty Sessional Courts for over 100 years, before they were moved to the new Courthouse on West Bars in 1965. An entrance to the slipper baths can be seen off South Street.

Knifesmithgate in the 1920s. Property on the north side has been partly removed to make way for road widening and later the 'Vic Arches'. Stokes original paint shop is still there as is the King's Head beyond, and the remains of the Olivers' foundry are still standing on the left.

Knifesmithgate in the early 1930s. Road widening is proceeding apace and the well known colonnade is almost complete. Stokes old building has gone, they have relocated under the arches on the extreme left. With the exception of Tinley's Corner the south side is almost as we know it today even if the businesses have changed.

West Bars in 1964. The old LDEC station is still standing, and the Market Hall, with the original cupola in place, has some time to go before reburbishment. The old Wm. Urton ironmongery awaits demolition opposite the Portland Hotel.

Cavendish Street around 1934. Site clearance has begun to make way for the new Regal cinema, Cavendish House offices and associated shops. The new Tinley's Shoe Shop and Kings Head on Knifesmithgate can be seen over the site.

Cavendish Street, *c.* 1934. An open site becomes a temporary car park before Cavendish House is erected, and Brampton brewery's new King's Head stands proudly on the other side of Broad Pavement. The trolleybus overheads would be there until 1938, when motor buses took over this Brampton-Whittington route.

It seems the shell of the new cinema has almost been completed by Kirk's workers, who can be seen on-site, indicating that the photograph was taken on a working day. If so, the road is unusually free of traffic. Greaves furniture showroom can be seen on the other side of Broad Pavement.

The western end of Knifesmithgate in around 1934, before it was extended to Rose Hill. The property in the centre was removed, leaving the Welbeck Inn and the Soresby Street chapel flanking the new road leading to the future Town Hall.

Broad Pavement, around 1932, shows a depressing aspect before most of the buildings were demolished for the Regal cinema, offices and shops. Only the property at the extreme end of the lane still survives.

High Street in the early part of the century, before the tram tracks were laid in 1904 and horse-drawn transport still ruled. The four-wheeled hansom cabs, known as 'growlers', await fares from the Angel Hotel and the Westminster Bank on the left.

Burlington Street, *c.* 1910, and trams are now in operation between Brampton terminus and Whittington Moor. Horsepower would last much longer though and one is drawing a cart full of beer crates into the cellars of J.B. White through what is now the entrance to the Golden Fleece.

Burlington Street in 1937 and a Straker-Clough trolleybus proceeds westwards on an almost clear highway. Although the shops have changed, the north-side buildings still survive, but those on the south side have all been replaced in what is now a pedestrian area.

Holywell Street, c. 1907. Eyre's furniture store has yet to extend to Cavendish Street and the Bluebell Inn will exist in its present form for another nineteen years. The building under demolition was the Moulders Arms, a Home Brewery pub which pulled its last pint in 1906.

Cavendish Street corner, *c.* 1934. The Blue Bell, owned by the Mansfield Brewery, operated normally whilst its successor was erected behind it as part of the cinema and office development.

Holywell Street in the mid-1930s can be dated by the overheads for trolleybuses. The long established fruiterer J.W. Damms owned much of the adjacent property, of which one shop was leased to David Osinski who became better known as Montague Burton.

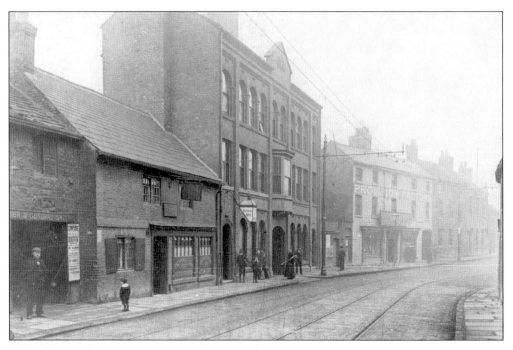

Holywell Street in the early 1900s when the trams still operated. The smithy on the left dates from the seventeenth century, and next door is the Exchange Inn which closed in 1909. William Glossop built the three story block for his solicitors business and leased a part to Gilmour's Brewery as the Victoria Hotel. The site was previously owned by the Duke of Devonshire.

The Market Place in the early 1980s. The photograph was taken from a window in Littlewoods Department Store when Marks & Spencer was being renovated and the old block opposite, recently vacated by Boots, was being refurbished for new tenants.

Tontine Road was redeveloped in the 1980s and adjacent property with it. The old established Greaves' Chemist had the famous long window removed, but replaced it with a modern facsimile before moving out to Vicar Lane to make way for Boots. The old window has been preserved.

Looking along Vicar Lane in the 1930s, showing the well-used St James' Hall. 'Jimmy's', as it was affectionately known, was the venue for regular – very temperate – dances, and was also the headquarters of the 2nd Chesterfield (Parish church) Scout Troop.

Chesterfield Market, c. 1910. This area was laid out in the thirteenth century and once had stone quarried from it to pave local streets and sidewalks. Most of the buildings, seen in this view from the market hall balcony, have survived, the exceptions being the Three Tuns pub next to Greaves' Chemist and the house above Duttons.

The market place must have had a pollution problem in the early part of the century when occupied by cattle and horses, and maybe this prompted the opening of a new cattle market to the south. The new Westminster bank would remain until 1968 but the old Town Hall site, used by Scales, was replaced by another bank in 1913.

Church Walk, 1916. This damaged plate negative seems to be the only record of the fire which destroyed the upper floors of the original Ryland Works. Most of the remaining walls were removed for safety reasons and never replaced. The damage was reported at £20,000 – a considerable sum at that time.

St Mary's Gate, c. 1916. The east facing wall of the fire-damaged building can be seen to the right, and more of it was removed later leaving only the ground floor usable. At the end of the century a night club was established there.

Rose Hill around 1930. This had stood on this fine site since 1730 and was built by the Thornhill family. Several owners occupied it, including a Hunloke family agent, Alderman John Brown. Demolition took place in 1936 for the present Town Hall site and gardens.

Rose Hill, 1936/37. The house is almost down and the grounds are being cleared for the laying of the Shentall Gardens and, to the west, the present Magistrates Court.

1936 and the Mayor, Alderman H.P. Short, is being photographed with fellow members of the Corporation on the occasion of laying the foundation stone of the new Town Hall. The bewigged official to the left is the Town clerk Richard Clegg.

1938, with the new Town Hall almost complete and the Shentall Gardens marked out. Many of the trees were removed to form the garden approach, but the two largest would survive to the 1990s. The overheads for the trolleybus are still in place at this time.

The new building stands well in the centre of immaculate lawns and flower beds with the Rural District Council offices to the north and the football stand beyond. Designed by Bradshaw, Gass & Hope, it was opened by the Duchess of Devonshire in April 1938 and cost £142,500.

Elder Way in the late 1920s. The Knifesmithgate development is in place and all the old property will soon go to build the modern road to Saltergate. Crow & Sons moved their warehouse to Union Walk, north of Glumangate.

Elder Way, a few weeks after the previous picture. Demolition is proceeding but not yet complete, and motorists have yet again taken advantage of a spare piece of ground. Barclays bank seems to be trading already.

The east side of Elder Way, c. 1933, and the old houses, four in number though still apparently occupied, would soon be removed for new offices on the site. A new entrance to the Unitarian chapel would be driven through to the road.

The new chapel gates mentioned previously have been installed and the Elder Way road has been surfaced, but much demolition remains to be done. The cottages on the left would have had poor light when the way was just a narrow footpath.

Knifesmithgate in the early 1930s. Old property is going to create space for a passage to Burlington Street and, alongside, the new Golden Fleece public house.

George Mason began producing tobacco in a factory on Wheeldon Lane off Low Pavement and as the business prospered became wealthy, moving to the old silk mill at Spital. Although producing nationally popular brands of cigarettes, chewing and pipe tobacco, the giants of the industry forced the firm into decline, Mason Junior selling out. The mill, photographed in 1996, is now owned by Spital Tile Co.

Infirmary Road, c. 1950. These eight 'Eventide Homes for Gentlewomen' were the gift of Alderman Edward Eastwood and built by William Rhodes. The tenants, who had to be 'aged gentlewomen of some slight means', had to furnish the dwellings, which were removed in the mid-1970s.

Chesterfield Workhouse and offices, *c.* 1900. Standing on Newbold Road, opposite Trinity church, the redbrick and stone edifice had its first 'deserving poor' residents admitted by the Board of Guardians in 1839. For much of its life the institution was under-used and, after other recent occupants, was demolished to make way for modern apartment blocks.

Scarsdale Hospital around 1912. Built in 1902 on Newbold Road, to the west of the workhouse, it was designed by the London firm of Scott & Moffatt. Intended to serve the 'poor of Chesterfield', it later serviced the whole community including geriatric and maternity care. It was demolished at the end of the century for new residential buildings.

The Shambles, *c*. 1916. This is the centre of the three yards running north to south. The Royal Oak on the left is still trading, but the Bulls Head on the right had its licence transferred to the Mason's Arms on Chatsworth Road in 1917. The stonework on the extreme left of the photograph is the old Yorkshire Penny Bank, now the Halifax PLC.

Holywell Street in the early 1930s. The Picture House was opened in September 1923 together with its own restaurant and ballroom. Acquired by the Oscar Deutsch circuit, it became the Odeon in 1938 and was later owned by Rank. It closed in October 1981 and the council bought it in 1987, renaming it The Winding Wheel.

The Bold Rodney Yard. This photograph is undated but is thought to be in the early 1930s. Older residents have recalled that occupation by gypsies was not uncommon, similarly funfairs. The building on the right is the Mount Zion church, Chatsworth Road.

Wheatbridge Road in 1995, just before demolition of the century-old box factory. A retail park has now been built on the site.

Stephenson Place, c. 1916. The new bank and Furness Chambers opposite still survive but the shops on Holywell Street were soon to go to provide a site for the new cinema – the Picture House, in the early 1920s.

Chesterfield from the west in the first decade of the century, recorded by Charles Robinson from the water tower seen opposite. Wright's pottery is to the left and Rose Hill and West House estates at the top, the LDEC goods shed and station are on the other side of West Bars.

Walton Road in the 1930s. Most of the property seen here has disappeared for road widening and redevelopment, mostly residential, but a supermarket filling station is now opposite the old one. They do not sell Shellmex petrol at 1/5 per gallon. ($7\frac{1}{2}$ pence).

Boythorpe Road, c. 1933. A photograph taken before the road widening operations. The level crossing of the Brampton spur remained into the 1950s and the kilns on the right were part of Edward Wright's pottery.

Horns Bridge in the early 1920s, before the stone arch was removed and a steel one put in its place to widen the road to Hasland. The A61 goes under the LDEC line to Derby.

The road to Hasland and beyond has much improved by the early 1930s. Traffic islands have arrived and pedestrians are now catered for.

Horns Bridge in May 1932. This low lying area of the town was always prone to flooding, and when over two inches of rain fell in a few hours it became impassable. None of these buildings survive today after the installation of the M1 link roundabout.

Lordsmill Street in the early 1930s. Taken from under the rail bridge carrying the Brampton spur, this photograph shows mostly residences which would be swept away in the 1960s and 1970s.

Lordsmill Street, *c.* 1921. The presence of the old Anchor Inn, on the right, dates this picture prior to 1923 and the new Ship Inn, on the corner of Hollis Lane, is under construction.

A damaged shot, probably by Nadin, of Lordsmill Street, in around 1916, showing Vicar Lane to the left and the very old properties on the main route to the town.

St Mary's Gate, c. 1910. A good, if vignetted, view of the narrow cobbled streets of the time, built for the use of steel tyres. Francis Glossop's long established business is to the right, and in the centre is the Hare and Greyhound, whose licensee was Mrs Betsy Renshaw. The pub was rebuilt in 1923 and sold by the John Smith Brewery in 1977. It then became a free house but closed in 1994 after the name changed, despite Church protests, to the Saint Inn. It is now owned and run as a community centre by the Parish church.

The south-west of the town, *c.* 1960. Taken from the old permanent way of the LDEC station, this view shows the rooftops from a rare angle. Prominent is the old police and fire station, with what is thought to be a hose-drying tower in the old Theatre Yard.

Beetwell Street, *c.* 1937. All the buildings in the foreground were removed for development which was delayed by the war and the sites were vacant for the duration. Jack Boult built a garage on the corner site in the late 1950s.

Lordsmill Street in the 1960s. Property marked for demolition included the infamous Markham Hostel (bed for two shillings a night), and a popular chip shop. The Crown Hotel closed in 1966, its licence transferred to the Badger at Brockwell. Boult's garage has now been erected on the Beetwell Street corner.

Beetwell Street, c. 1935. The buildings beyond the Prince of Wales public house were removed on both sides of the road. The pub itself went after closure in the 1960s, as did the nearer properties; a new multi-storey car park is there now.

The south-west end of Vicar Lane in the early 1930s. Most of the south side was redeveloped when the new 1934 bus station was erected, and only the Commercial Hotel survived to the 1970s.

The south-east corner of Central Pavement in the late 1920s or early 1930s. Roe's Chemist went, together with Edges Printers, who relocated on Low Pavement. Vicar Lane was thus opened up to traffic instead of the footpath past the Commercial Hotel.

Opposite: Church Alley in the late 1930s. Few pictures exist of this very old row of cottages backing onto the churchyard. Just off the frame to the right is the 'Old Crooked Spire', a Brampton Brewery pub demolished in 1930 along with the cottages to construct Church Way. The new Crooked Spire public house was rebuilt alongside the old.

A 1995 view up the spire from the tower top showing the herringbone pattern of the fifty tons of lead sheathing. The cock weathervane measures 2ft 9ins from beak to tail and stands 6ft 8ins above the spire top. The cardinal arms, each 5ft 8ins long, were a gift from the Markham Co.

Looking up the inside of the crooked spire at some of the forty-eight tons of wood which are not even attached to the tower. The serious fire of December 1961 almost reached these timbers before it was controlled.

41

A view of Alpine Gardens from a tram top in the 1920s. This feature, donated by T.P. Wood, was made possible by the removal of Dr Greene's house which blocked the end of Burlington Street. The north end of Church Alley may be seen on the right.

The west end of Spa Lane, *c.* 1905, with possibly a Scarsdale Brewery dray coming from the brewery below. Two pubs at the corners, the Phoenix to the right (rebuilt 1924) and the Plough to the left, said to be 'a house of the lowest order'. The County Court now stands on the Plough site.

Two

Getting About

West Bars in 1914. Ezra Coates pauses his No. 8 prussian blue and primrose tram on a rather dirty road, with a shiny booted young conductor. This service operated between Walton Lane and the market place from 1881 to 1904, the Corporation buying the Company for £2,050 and operating it from November 1897 at a penny a journey.

A tram has reached the town terminus at the market place and has reversed the car on its chassis by walking the horses round. There was a loop line on West Bars where the trams could pass each other. Revenue in the last year of operation was £46 per week and wages £14 per week.

The ill-fated Lancashire Derbyshire and East Coast Railway in 1906. It operated from Chesterfield to Pyewipe Junction, near Lincoln, failing in its aim to link Warrington with Sutton-on-Sea.

Chesterfield, 1903. Built to draw revenue mainly from coal traffic, the LDEC operated a considerable passenger service and even carried royalty. Here No. 26 has been specially prepared at Chesterfield to convey Edward VII from Tuxford to Ollerton for Welbeck Abbey.

The LDEC station, West Bars, c. 1900. Looking new but without the clock, and seemingly with a train due, from the 'growler' cabs waiting. From the outset, capital was lacking and the company was taken over by the Great Central railway in 1907. Fifty years later the line ceased operations from the town and the building went in the 1960s.

Midland Station, 1905. This Gothic-styled station was designed by the MR architect Neill and erected in the 1870s. After an unsatisfactory refurbishment, a new station was built in the late 1990s.

The GC Station, c. 1910. This delightful wooden building dated from 1892, built by the Manchester, Sheffield & Lincolnshire Railway for its loop line from Heath to Staveley. Taken over by the Great Central in 1897, it operated till 1967. The inner relief road now occupies the site.

A trip in a charabanc in the1920s. Good weather and even roads were necessary for an outing to the seaside in the open-topped, solid-tyred coaches.

The coming of the trams, 1904, and track-laying is taking place on Sheffield Road adjacent to the old Grammar School and the Rendezvous skating rink.

Delivery of a tram body, 1905. So the caption to this photograph indicates, but although the style of livery (in black and white) matches that on local trams, this body seems shorter than those in contemporary pictures. An interesting image, nevertheless.

No. 4 tram stops for the camera on Burlington Street, in around 1905. The service began in December 1904 between Brampton and the 'Jug and Glass' at Whittington, with cars supplied by the Brush Co.

A decorated Daimler Fleetline in 1982 in a Town Hall car park. After a procession around Chesterfield to celebrate the centenary of public transport in the town, the coaches went on display for the day. The old No. 8 horse tram seen on page 43, now restored after many years use as a summerhouse, was also included.

Early transport, Hasland, c.1910. Has the car, thought to be a Renault, stalled on the hill, broken down or just starting? The sight was enough to attract a group of onlookers to Eyre Street.

West Bars around 1927. The Brampton to West Bars Service was the first route operated by the new Straker–Clough trolleybuses which were numbered 1 to 15 despite there being only fourteen vehicles – No. 13 being omitted!

Stephenson Place in the early 1930s, and an almost new Ransomes Sims & Jeffries D2 double-decker passes Singer's Corner on its way to Brampton Terminus. The last trolleybus ran on 24 March 1938 before petrol engines took over. Sadly, none of these trackless electrics was preserved.

In 1932, following demonstrations at the Tube Works attended by the Mayor (Alderman T.D. Sims) and Corporation, a seven year old Bristol four tonner was converted to run on towns gas. The fuel was carried in Tube Co. cylinders under the body when a trial service on Saturdays to Storforth Lane took place. Insufficient gas could be carried to last all day, however, and the experiment was abandoned.

The pneumatic tyred Bristol thirty-one seater NU 7907, seen at an unidentified filling station in 1932/3. The compression and governing equipment was supplied by Bryan Donkin Co., and on 9 February 1933 a successful trial to Rotherham was undertaken.

Chesterfield Thornfield depot in 1936, and a row of fine looking Leyland Tiger single and Titan double-deckers are lined up for the camera.

Vicar Lane in the late 1990s, and the 1934 bus station stands forlornly empty as it awaits demolition for the new development. British Home Stores has now taken its site.

Three

The Forties and After

New Square in 1954, Dents and the old Star and Garter buildings have another few years before redevelopment. Traffic still travels up to the post office and Burlington Street, just about bisecting the square otherwise filled with stalls.

The Market Place, 1978. The stalls are the same and many of the traders are in the same positions, but all the Low Pavement names have changed although the well-known façades were saved to preserve the character of the area.

Low Pavement, 1979/80. The fronts are supported but work is going on behind them to build the Pavements complex. The topless market hall is also being refurbished and augmented.

The Market Hall in April 1979, and the camera can see through the gutted ground floor to the AGD building on West Bars.

New Beetwell Street, 1979. The empty properties fronting onto Low Pavement await careful removal before the 'Pavements' take their place. It was here that the short-lived Corporation-run Civic Restaurant operated in the early 1950s.

The Market Place in the mid-1960s. Yellow lines have made their appearance and many of the properties here and on Burlington Street will go forever. T.P. Woods colonnade and the buildings either side are ready for demolition. Littlewoods will move in and Marks & Spencer will extend westwards.

Burlington street in the 1940s, and probably Sunday lunchtime from the shadows and lack of people. This angle of view shows the narrow pavement on the south side at a time when two-way traffic used this road.

Market Place in the 1980s. Taken from Littlewoods store on a summer market day, this view echoes what T.P. Wood would have seen from his office nearly 100 years ago: cobblestones then but no traffic warden!

Vicar Lane, *c.* 1980. John Turner, then owned by the Courtauld Group, would soon retire from the town and the Fine Fare store would later become Wilkinson's. The property beyond went in the 1990s but the oldest building, to the right, survives as a building society.

Vicar Lane in August 1998 and the shops are still trading, although the bus station has gone. The Wilkinson Group has decided to open on Sundays and would survive the imminent development.

Tontine Road in the early 1980s. All the property south of Markham Road has now gone and the fine footbridge has become superfluous, as have most of the bus shelters. Beyond, Chesterfield Cylinders and Bryan Donkin are due to cut back or cease manufacturing here, as is the Avenue plant on the skyline.

Station Road, 1983. From the church tower it can be seen that nature is taking over in the once busy Shentall Warehouse. The old Heathcote house is to the left and the *Derbyshire Times* top right. St Mary's court now occupies the Shentall site.

The police and fire stations in the 1920s. The larger building with the sliding doors housed the fire appliances and ambulances, also the police cars. Tontine Road had still to be developed to the market place.

Tontine Road in the 1930s. The new police headquarters is complete and the road, which will be undisturbed until the 1980s, has a new Barkers store on Low Pavement corner. This would later become McDonalds.

In the early 1980s Tontine Road became a footpath before the Pavements development was complete. The 1937 police station and adjoining buildings are being removed to create space for the new library.

New Beetwell Street in October 1982. Foundations for the new County Library are in progress, and Tontine Road to the north has become a goods entrance to the Pavements. The police headquarters are now on the old Beetwell Street.

Saltergate, c. 1955. An aspect recorded perhaps to illustrate the traffic hazard of the leaning plane trees, especially to high buses. They would go, together with all the property on the left and much on the right side, including the old offices of the Staffordshire Farmers.

Saltergate, *c.* 1955. Looking west to Elder Way, the two corners of which were razed in the 1930s and stood vacant during the war years.

An early 1980s view of Saltergate. The whole area to the right is now given over to a vast car park, and is an island following the construction of a new road to Holywell Street. The Co-op has built on both corners of Elder Way, and the stone entrance to the Elder Yard chapel is the only surviving building.

Broad Pavement in the late 1970s. Once known as Narrow Lane, this street once held long queues for the cheaper seats at the Regal cinema, and has been redeveloped beyond Greaves' furniture showroom on the left.

Knifesmithgate, 1953. A George Martin photograph taken from the rooms of the Photographic Society on Stephenson Place one sunny–Saturday?–morning. No yellow lines or no-parking signs, two-way traffic and the Kings Head still owned and supplied by the Brampton Brewery.

Saltergate in the late 1970s. The largest car park in the town, photographed from the top of yet another car park. The ancient stone of the church is being cleaned and temporary shops are in Shepley's Yard till they can be re-housed.

From the same viewpoint as above, showing that popular phenomenon, the car-boot sale, held each Sunday and organized by the Corporation.

The Wesleyan church, Saltergate, well-cleaned in the early 1980s. The original building dates from 1795 and was extended in 1822 with recent refurbishment. The wooden hut to its right was the headquarters for a generation of the 25th Chesterfield Cubs, Scouts and Guides.

Wheeldon Lane, 1978. Once one of the main ways from town to the South and river, this narrow lane accessed several industries from lace-making to tobacco manufacture. The steps led to New Beetwell Street and there was a similar flight on the other side on the way to the market place.

West Bars Roundabout in the 1970s. To create this island, many properties were cleared, mostly old cottages numbering around fifty. In the next thirty years, most of the remaining buildings will be cleared. The old Brampton Brewery, with the billboards, houses Auto-windscreens and will be replaced by the huge red B&Q store. The house on the corner of Wheatbridge Road gave way to a short-lived filling station before, together with the Co-op milk depot and Robinsons Wheatbridge Mills, being replaced by a retail park. Quite who was expected to cross a busy road to sit on the seats, later put in the middle of the island, is a mystery. The now fully grown trees change the whole aspect of the island today.

Brampton Brewery in the early 1970s. The second of the three breweries in the town to close down, this one had operated from this building since 1905 and was said to be the first electrically operated brewery in the country. It was taken over by Warwicks in March 1955, and the last brew was made in June of that year.

The Queen's Park Hotel opened in 1913 as the Three Tuns Inn, changing its name in 1915. Together with other property on Markham Road, it was demolished speedily in 1997 to increase car parking space in the retail park.

The Red Lion, Vicar Lane, *c.* 1980. Rebuilt in 1920 adjacent to its original position to facilitate road improvements, this Stones pub was closed in 1989 in anticipation of the extensive redevelopment of the area.

The Devonshire Arms, Holywell Street, *c.* 1930. This Tennants pub, dating from the early 1800s, closed its doors in 1957 when its landlord, M. Drinkwater, transferred to the Whitecotes Inn together with the licence.

Beetwell Street in the 1980s. A row of portakabins was erected for shops to carry on trading whilst property was demolished to clear sites for the new Vicar Lane development. The rear of the new stores and a large car park now occupy this space.

Holywell Street in 1958. All the once elegant buildings were removed in the 1970s. Together with the space created by the demolition of those on Saltergate, the biggest car park in the town was formed.

The Chesterfield Window in St Mary's was donated by public subscription to commemorate the 750th anniversary of the church. It traces the town's history and industrial growth. Notice the spire before it became crooked!

The pomegranate was used as the Common Seal of the town until 1974, and appeared on official documents, corporation buses etc. The use of this fruit is thought to be unique and may have connections with Catherine of Aragon. This image is on a uniform badge.

The new Armorial Bearings of the Borough granted by the College of Arms includes a pomegranate tree, a Derby ram and a cock and pynot (magpie), the latter being a reminder of the local plotting in an inn of that name, which led to the 'Glorious Revolution' of 1688. The motto is an obvious pun on our famous landmark.

The Rendezvous roller skating rink, c. 1980. For many years a corn mill owned and operated by the Burkitts, it was adapted for roller skating, and used for many other pursuits including boxing matches and dog shows, finishing a useful life as a mattress warehouse.

Chesterfield Magistrates Court in the 1990s. Taken on one of the Court open days, this shows the bench in No. 1 Court. The building on West Bars was designed by Professor Allen to resemble two open law books standing spine to spine, and was opened by Lord Denning in 1965.

The Courthouse in spring 1995. It has four permanent courtrooms, necessary offices – and cells. Black and white outside, it has aroused equally opposing opinions as to its aesthetic qualities. It will become redundant when a new, larger court is opened in the new century.

Stephenson Memorial Hall, 1990. A view that may not be seen again for a long time. The photograph was taken over the debris from the demolition of Shentalls Warehouse on Station Road and shows the museum (left), the Pomegranate Theatre, and the old Heathcote house – now a restaurant. Office blocks (St Mary's Court) now fill the site.

The Town Hall, *c.* 1960. Although the southern aspect of the Town Hall is more visible these days, it seems a pity that the two old trees had to go for safety reasons. But did you notice?

Dunston Lane in the early 1950s. The houses seen at the Littlemoor end were completed as the war began, but housing estates now cover all the area shown.

Church Way, 1999. As the century ended, the seeming symbols of the age, the tower cranes, came to town to create a new precinct between Burlington Street and Beetwell Street. How long will that last?

Four
Trading Places

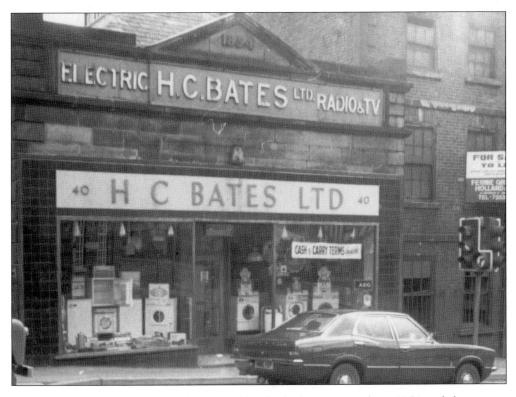

Scarsdale Vaults around 1970. The Dunnells rebuilt this wine vault in 1854 and their name could be seen in stone behind the Bates sign. The Bates brothers kept a similar shop a few doors up Lordsmill Street for many years.

Bates Shop traded for many years at this address, next to the Phoenix pub in the golden age of radio. J.J. Shorts later moved to Stephenson Place, dealing mainly in mens' clothing for over fifty years before closing in the 1990s.

The wine vaults in the late 1970s. The Dunnells' sign can now be seen with the Bates heading gone; Comet used the shop until they moved to Saltergate in the 1980s. The old Scarsdale Brewery offices are being restored next door.

THOS. FURNESS & SON,

M.P.S.,

DISPENSING CHEMISTS,

The Pharmacy, Knifesmith Gate,

CHESTERFIELD.

Physicians' Prescriptions Dispensed
at lowest prices, consistent with best
Drugs and careful compounding.

THOMAS FURNESS, L.D.S.,

Thomas Furness kept the chemist shop in the block he built, calling the building 'Furness Chambers', on Stephenson Place. He later qualified as a dentist. His sons did likewise and Claude had a surgery next to the shop, run by Tom Junior, an MPS. Thomas Senior died in 1912 just before the long block was completed.

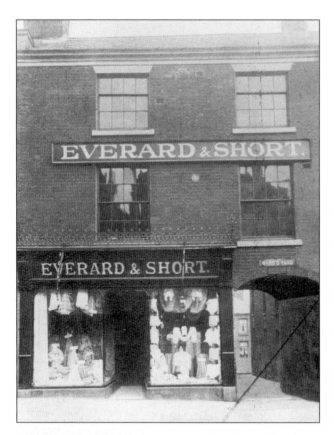

Central Pavement, *c.* 1912. Walter Everard and William Short were selling drapery and ladies' garments in the nineteenth century until their deaths in 1919. The shop currently sells greetings cards.

Central Pavement in the late 1920s, with the window dressed, possibly for one of the town's shopping festivals. The Maypole Dairy Co., together with nearby Liptons, closed in 1971, citing excessive rate increases.

Brampton Brewery, c. 1900. A group of grim faced employees seemingly from the manager down to the errand lads. They would probably move into the new brewery, opened in 1905, following a fire at the old one.

Clayton's Tannery, 1908. This was a family business, founded by Joseph Clayton in 1840 on Spa Lane and later at Clayton Street off Hollis Lane. This works expanded to cover three acres before it was destroyed by a serious fire in 1913. The company still survives however at the century's end. The photograph shows the shaving room.

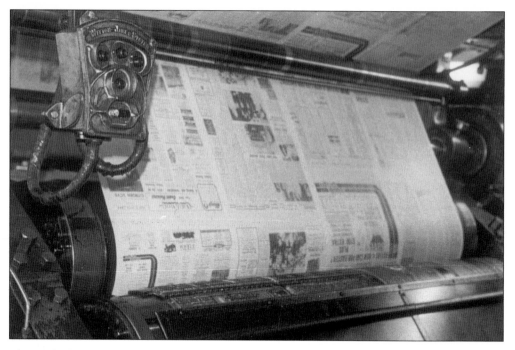

The *Derbyshire Times* rolling off the press in the 1970s. At this time the paper was in broadsheet and used the hot metal process for printing. Founded in 1854 by Francis A. Hatton, it was printed in Angel Yard, off Packers' Row, up to 1857.

Munitions in wartime. The label on this photograph suggests that the ladies are working for the war effort at Sheepbridge, but at which part of the works is not specified. The only men in the picture seem to be just onlookers!

The market place in the early 1920s. Sampson and Barfoot, once shop assistants here, bought the business in 1885. Barfoot opened his own shop elsewhere and Sampson later sold the business to F.W. Dutton.

Market Place in the 1970s. Wakefields came here in the 1950s, moving from their small shop on Packers' Row. They expanded in both directions and traded until the Abbey National Bank occupied the site in 1993.

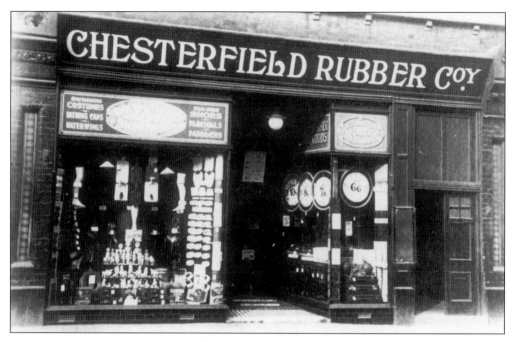

Stephenson Place, *c.* 1936. The Chesterfield Rubber Company occupied two sites on Cavendish Street before moving here in the mid-1930s, selling Indian rubber goods, waterproofs and raincoats, both retail and wholesale.

Stephenson Place around 1912. This building, adjacent to Dr Greene's house at the end of Burlington Street, was the retail shop of W. M. F. Taylor for many years. On completion of Furness Chambers (seen roofless behind), the business took premises to the right of Nottingham House and traded until the 1960s.

Knifesmithgate, c. 1935. Tinley's shoe shop in the throes of rebuilding the premises in which they would trade to the 1990s. The business was started by W.M. Tinley in the 1800s.

New Square, c. 1910. These premises were occupied by Dr Stokes, an eminent botanist, in the 1800s, and were later to become a bank to the present day. The Sheffield Banking Co. altered the façade, and later the National Provincial Bank operated there. It was occupied for a time by the National Westminster Bank and is currently the Yorkshire Bank.

White's showroom number two, *c.* 1920. Joseph White founded the musical instrument and furniture stores on Corporation Street in the 1800s, and it continued trading through to the 1970s. The showroom reflects the popularity in home musical entertainment in pre-radio times.

Tapton Lane around 1915. Why Whites label their Cabinet works as 'electric' is unknown, unless they were pioneers of electric light in those days!

Knifesmithgate around 1935. J.K. Swallow & Sons had prospered after moving from the South side of Burlington Street, rebuilding the whole west end of the block, and would shortly extend to include J.W. Clough's site, building an arcade there.

Burlington Street, 1970. The popular department store closed in 1970 and as Swallows had redeveloped the entire end of this block, so would the new owners to provide rented shops.

Hasland, *c.* 1920. The Co-op (to use its popular name) opened its doors in Chesterfield on 23 August 1894 in New Square. Talks went on for nineteen years before the separate Hasland branch was amalgamated with the town shop.

Chatsworth Road, *c.* 1912. Founded in the 1800s, this well-known butcher traded as Scott & Haslam to the 1940s on the corner of Walton Fields Road. It would appear to be Yuletide judging by the holly.

Cavendish Street, 1950. The staff of the well-known hairdresser pose for the camera. From left to right they are: Don Tilley, Richard T. Howes (the owner who took over in 1946), Horace Gratton and George Alberts. The business is currently under the proprietorship of David Howes.

Ryland Works, c. 1945. This huge warehouse was erected, probably in the 1920s, to replace the much smaller one destroyed by the 1916 fire in Church Walk. It flourished as a builders' supplier until the 1990s.

Burlington Street around 1905. The Taylor Brothers were perhaps the premier store for drapery in the town, especially for mourning clothes, after acquiring the business from Hewitt & Heane. Their premises extended from the market place to Irongate.

Boots cash chemist came to the town in 1895 at No. 3 Market Place, and extended throughout the top of this block as vacancies occurred. But it was not until after the war, when Redfern's Grocers and Meeson's Sweets went, that they occupied the whole High Street end.

Ashgate Road, *c.* 1912. John Heywood Gregory ran a thriving confectionery business at No. 13 High Street, his pony and trap was photographed delivering at a rather dirty Ashgate Road.

Samuel Elliott's Sweet shop, High Street, 1912. This display won first prize in the shopping festival of that year. Elliott had a factory in Park Road at that time and later manufactured at Quarry Lane in Brampton. The business, founded in 1892, ceased in 1959.

Burlington Street in the 1950s. This long, narrow store, between Dewhurst's butcher and Frisby's shoe shop, was a drapery business owned by Peter Murphy & Sons in the 1920s. It was known locally as 'The Beehive' because of the sign which hung over the pavement for many years.

Brampton Coliseum, c. 1920. An old Methodist chapel, it was said to be one of the first cinemas in 1907, and still had wooden pews in the 1930s. Refurbished after a 1939 fire, the comfortable 600 seat theatre lasted into the television age, closing in 1957. It is now a car showroom.

South Street. William Britt & Sons was founded around 1818 and traded in the same place for over 160 years, closing down as the street redevelopment began in the 1980s.

Burlington Street in the early 1990s. The imposing, but relatively short-lived, façade of Woolworths did not last much longer, being removed to create 'Steeplegate', a road to Vicar Lane in the 1990s scheme. The store has been in the town since 1932 and is now situated to the south, on the new Vicar Lane.

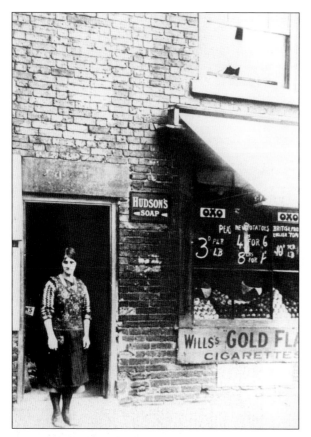

Chatsworth Road in the late 1920s or early 30s has Emily Blakemore outside her small greengrocers at No. 135 Chatsworth Road. In the pre-supermarket days, these tiny outlets on many street corners made for genuine 'convenience shopping'.

Derby Road, 1988. An unusual angle of view to the NCB Avenue Coke plant at Wingerworth. Designed to carbonise coal and process the by-products for twenty odd years, it worked for over twice that length of time before closing in the 1990s.

Five
Occasions and People

THE LATE ALDERMAN T. P. WOOD.

THE DEPUTY MAYOR OF CHESTERFIELD.
(ALD. C. P. MARKHAM.)

T.P. Wood, left, and C.P. Markham, right. There have been no more generous public benefactors to the town than these two worthy gentlemen. Both born locally, the former was a wine merchant who caused the Queen's Park to be laid, the latter an industrialist, who removed the notorious 'Dog Kennels' at his own expense. Both men served as Mayor three times.

A parade up Lordsmill Street in the early part of the century, showing children and members of the Ragged School. The occasion was probably a Whitsunday Walk. The Phoenix pub is on the left and Dunnell's Vault a little below.

Brimington in the 1920s. This photograph shows the Brimington boys football team being drawn round the village on a four horse wagonette, with plenty of sightseers to cheer the team and view the (Clayton?) shield behind the driver.

From the trim appearance of the engine and its crew, this occasion in around 1912 was more likely to have been a practice than a real fire. The solid tyred Merryweather could attend fires at 50mph and, when there, pump water at the rate of 450 gallons per minute.

But the balloon did go from the Queen's Park in August 1906, taking Eustace Short and Henry Barker to Rotherham. The famous Short brothers spent their youth in Old Whittington and later founded the aircraft company. A copy of a letter from Hugh Oswald Short is on the next page.

Gillhams Farm
Lynchmere
Nr Haslemere
Surrey
Sept 19 1956

The Editor
Staveley News
Chesterfield Derbyshire

Dear Sir
Many thanks for sending me the Staveley News. Naturally I was interested in your article entitled "The Balloon that did." I can well remember the event. I knew Tom Wardle very well. His father was once the Mayor of Chesterfield. But none of the Wardles went up that day. It was the late Mr Henry Barker who went up with my brother Eustace. Henry Barker was my cousin on my mother's side. I made my first balloon ascent in 1898. Eustace learned to fly when he was 52, and flew in the roughest weather. Six years later he was dying in the air from a heart attack, but managed to land opposite our works. In 1910 at Rochester I invented a new method of aircraft construction which is called all metal stressed skin construction, now in universal use for all giant aircraft, such as large Bombers, commercial aircraft, & fighter aircraft. The Short Sunderland built in 1933 is still in use. Some of them took part in the battles in Korea. It is not too much to say that this form of construction saved Gt Britain so far as battles in the air were concerned, in world war II. In 1942 my company was Nationalised by the late Sir Stafford Cripps. Since then I have retired with the title of Life President of Short Brothers & Harland Ltd Belfast. Again many thanks for sending me your Magazine

Yours sincerely
Hugh Oswald Short
Hon FRAeS.

In 1956 the *Staveley News*, house journal of the Staveley company, printed an article round the old picture of the balloon, sending a copy to the surviving Short brother. This is his reply.

The Sheepbridge Works football team 1919/20. The occasion is not specified and only a few faces can be identified, they are: W.M. Witham in the trilby; Draycott, the player standing on the left; Baker, the goalkeeper in large cap and Horace Wass, sitting at the far left, who later played over 400 games for Chesterfield FC.

Corporation Street, June 1906. A good escort to the station for the Duke of Devonshire, who had unveiled a memorial tablet to the Boer War fallen in the parish church. Both the Midland, left, and the Freemans Hotels were operating then.

Sheffield Road, October 1926. Coming down Stonegravels Hill the front axle gave way on this tram, derailing it to cause the pile-up seen here. No serious casualties resulted. Electric trams were phased out in 1927.

1926 and the Chesterfield radio society pose with their impressive array of equipment, possibly near the Bowling Green.

Chesterfield races, *c.* 1918, showing the grandstand, the starter's box and the frame. These meetings began in 1685 at the instigation of the Duke of Devonshire. Racecourse Road and Stand Road indicate the course of the track, which also took in part of Whittington. The last race was in 1924.

Eastwood Park, 1913. The Mayor, Ernest Shentall (Later Sir Ernest) with Alderman G.A. Eastwood, the donor, at the opening of the park at Hasland on 2 July. The Freedom of the Borough was conferred on Alderman Eastwood that same day.

The Civic Theatre around 1951. The Theatre, now The Pomegranate, was opened on 19 February 1949 by Kathleen Harrison. Weekly repertory followed, featuring many actors who became household names. The photograph shows Rowena Ingram and William Lucas.

Chesterfield St John Ambulance Brigade pose for the camera in 1950. The officer to the right is Lance Benson and the boy seated to his right is David Howes, the well-known hairdresser and local historian.

Windsor, 1949. A contingent of King's Scouts representing the county at the St George's Day Celebrations parade past the King, Queen and Princesses at Windsor Castle. These scouts were led by J.T. Franks, the Scout Master Of the 25th Chesterfield Troop (left).

Newbold, 1957, and the Duke of Devonshire opens the new Scout headquarters off Newbold Road, erected at a cost of £3,700. Derek Scattergood, Group Scout Master of the first Brimington troop, is nearest the Duke, with F.C. Greasby (DC), the Revd Handford and Ted Weston in attendance.

Home Guards, 1942. The 'B' Company of the local volunteer militia, which was acting as a Guides Section, was under the command of Assistant Platoon Commander CQM ERL (Peter) Powell, (centre, front).

ERL (Peter) Powell with some of his trophies gathered from around the world in his capacity as a leading official in national and international athletics. He also had a successful teaching career, becoming headmaster at Gilbert Heathcote and Dunston Schools. He died in 1990.

Hardwick Hall, *c.* 1952. A group of Chesterfield Photographic Society members on a visit to the stately home. Long time members were John and Elsie Cannam (front left), John Storer and George Martin (extreme right).

Low Pavement, 1994. A well-dressing at the Peacock Centre celebrates the 'Glorious Revolution' plotted at the Revolution House, Old Whittington, which resulted in the restoration of the monarchy.

Peacock exhibition in 1995. The Chesterfield Photographic Society exhibits the prints of members annually in this well restored floor of the Peacock Information Centre.

The Parish church, 22 December 1961. Great work by fifty firemen only just prevented a serious blaze in the north transept spreading to the belfry and spire. Even so, a unique organ was destroyed and damage of £40,000 resulted from the fire.

Chatsworth Road, 1997. Cup fever gripped the town when the local team reached the semi-finals of the FA Cup, even forcing a replay with a Premier League team before losing. The team toured the town on this bus to deserved acclaim.

Six
Schools and Scholars

Christ Church School, 1928. Mr A.C. Tonkin was headmaster at this time when the A-form posed for the camera. The school, just north of the town, was rebuilt in 1969, and opened by the Bishop of Repton on a site to the west of this one.

TAPTON HOUSE, NEAR CHESTERFIELD,

DERBYSHIRE,

The Seat of the late GEORGE STEPHENSON, Esq.

At the above Mansion, Young Ladies are Educated in every department of English and Continental Literature, and have secured to them all the advantages of a first-rate Establishment.

The system of instruction adopted is the result of extensive observation, and of many years' experience, and has been honored with uniform approbation. Its object is to develope the mental faculties,—to facilitate the acquisition of knowledge,—to excite a laudable ambition to excel,—to ensure the formation of correct habits,—and to combine all the advantages of a *home* education with the practical duties of a well regulated school.

The Misses Pocock and Walker,

in inviting the attention of Parents and Guardians to their establishment, beg to assure them that no effort will be spared to promote the religious and intellectual improvement of their pupils, and to merit a continuance of that confidence with which for several years they have been honored.—By their removal to the above capacious residence, they flatter themselves that they have secured accommodations rarely to be met with in educational establishments.

TAPTON HOUSE is situated on an eminence, in a most salubrious and beautiful part of Derbyshire; it is connected with extensive pleasure grounds, park, &c. and is furnished with baths, and every convenience for the promotion of health and comfort: and being contiguous to the Chesterfield Railway Station it presents the utmost facility of access to every part of the Kingdom.

TERMS:

Board and Education in the usual branches of English Literature, *Thirty-five Guineas per Annum;*
Junior Pupils, *Thirty Guineas.* Washing, *Three Guineas.*
French, *Four Guineas.* Latin, German, and Italian, each, *Six Guineas.*
Piano Forte and Singing, *Eight Guineas.* Harp and Guitar, each, *Eight Guineas.*
Drawing, in various styles, *Six Guineas.* Calisthenics and Deportment Exercises, &c. in the Winter Season.
Remaining the Vacation, *Three Guineas.* Daily Boarders, *Fourteen Guineas,*
Each Pupil to be provided with Towels, Table Napkins, a Silver Fork, Dessert and Tea Spoon,
which will be returned on leaving.

Three months' notice, or premium, is required prior to the removal of any young Lady
from the Family Circle.

Tapton House from the south-west, 1995. C.P. Markham moved to Ringwood Hall and gifted the house to the people of Chesterfield. Tapton House School was founded in 1931 with Harry Mellor MA as headmaster, becoming successful and well loved. The school closed in 1991 and is now a College of Further Education.

The Girls' High School, 1912. Later known as St Helena, it was opened by the Duke of Devonshire, having cost £24,000 and being the first purpose-built Girls' High School in the county. It was successful for nearly eighty years before closing due to reorganization in the 1990s.

Opposite: Tapton House, *c.* 1851. Built in the late-eighteenth century for the Chesterfield banker, Isaac Wilkinson, the House has seen many phases, notably the tenancy of George Stephenson, the Markham family and as a secondary school.

Founded in 1594, this boys 'Free Grammar School' building dates from 1846 and was extended later to the south and east. In the 1970s the school was rebuilt at Brookside in Brampton. Local policies later finished off the old school and it became co-educational in the 1990s. It is now a 'Community School'.

Boythorpe 1930/31. To cater for the large estate around it, William Rhodes Infant and Junior School, and later the Boys Modern, were built in the early 1930s and named after a local worthy, an ex-Mayor and Freeman of the borough.

Hasland, 1908. Neither the junior class of the Hasland Junior Council School nor their teachers look very pleased to face the camera, but their attire is interesting. Pinafore dresses and Eton collars are in vogue, as are ribbons in the hair. Sadly, no names are given.

Vicar Lane, *c.* 1920. The Victorian School, opened in 1845, commemorated the Queen's visit and was initiated by the Vicar, Thomas Hill. He provided a blue uniform for some pupils and it became known as the Blue Coat School. Some of these outfits may be seen on this form picture, taken before the school closed in the 1930s.

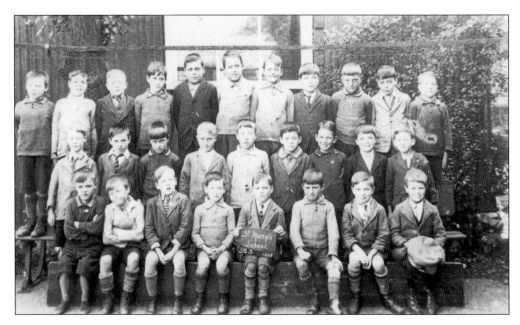

Spencer Street, 1921. The standard three in St Mary's Roman Catholic School was situated on Spencer Street at this time. The new Roman Catholic Mixed Modern School was erected on Cross Street and opened in July 1930.

Mary Swanwick, 1933. No names have been supplied with this photograph of the Mary Swanwick netball team of 1933, however the Schoolmaster is Mr C.C. Handford, who taught there for many years before becoming headmaster.

Seven

Curious Corners

Town Hall, 1980. This noble edifice, visible from miles around since 1938, is so familiar that people seldom notice the details.

Royal Hospital in the 1970s. Crowded around with annexes at this time, this 1859 building has been refurbished inside and out and stands in open spaces once again, almost a park. Sadly – a car park.

Stephenson Memorial Hall, 1980. A detail on a gable - is it a lightning conductor or just an ornamental finial?

Post office, 1982. Formerly the home of Gilbert Crompton, a banker, the building was opened in its present function in 1886, after moving from directly opposite.

Church Way in the 1970s. This rear aspect of the new Burlington Street faces down Packers' Row and had this multi-coloured chequered pattern. It has now lost some of its attractiveness and is all one shade.

Church Way, 1981. This striking elevation of excellent brickwork belonged not to a large hall but to the recently demolished Woolworth building.

Soresby Street, 1981. Well-weathered and eroded slightly, this corner of the Congregational chapel has endured the elements since 1823.

Knifesmithgate, 1977. This decorative carving stands over the front of what was once the entrance to the Victoria cinema and the colonnade fondly known as 'The Vic. Arches'.

Cavendish Street, 1978. In the heyday of the movies, this short tower was the apex of the Regal cinema, opened in 1936 to show the film *Follow the Fleet*, featuring Fred Astaire and Ginger Rogers.

Eyre chapel, 1997. Possibly dating from the thirteenth century, this small building stood derelict until restored by the Civic Society in 1987. The new windows commemorate the Eyre family (left), and Graham Robinson (right) who led the campaign to retain the town market in the 1970s.

Holywell Street, 1995. A highly decorative carving of the old Borough Seal was fixed to the new Maternity Home built in the 1920s behind the old hospital. It was used as a medical ward before closure in the 1980s.

Church Walk, 1994. This elaborate door frame was an entrance to the original Ryland Works, later Eyres used-furniture showroom. It is presently a night club.

Holywell Street, 1995. This good-as-new corner protector guided iron tyred wheels clear of the corner to prevent damage by the hubs. It was made at Spital Foundry, owned by the Wharton family.

South Street, 1995. The arms over Britts Shop had been upside down for perhaps 100 years and are, at last, in the right position. They are the arms of Sir Richard Westmacott RA, an eminent sculptor, some of whose work is on the Marble Arch and other places in London.

Knifesmithgate, 1970s. This well-carved trademark of the Brampton Brewery is seen outside the pub on the corner of Broad Pavement. When Brampton owned it, it was the King's Head and is now Boma's Bar.

Knifesmithgate, 1995. This grotesque head can be seen adjacent to the entrance of the Golden Fleece, there is another grimacing one on the other side.

Corporation Street, 1980. This decorative plasterwork, incorporating many musical instruments, can be seen adjoining the façade of the old White's building.

Glumangate, 1995. No. 30 on this ancient street was built in the Dutch gable style by William Rhodes in 1904. Miss Isabella Ann George operated a dress shop which traded here till the 1950s.

Burlington Street in the 1970s. One of the many cupolas in the town centre, this round one is on the Irongate Corner, over Boots main entrance. The windows below it are, unusually, of curved glass.

122

Eight
From on High

Wheatbridge Mill in the 1960s, probably photographed from the Brampton Brewery. The chimney was dismantled in 1973 and the tower in 1995. A retail park now occupies much of the foreground.

West Bars in the early 1960s. The biggest building in the town seems almost complete, but may not be occupied at this time. The extension of New Beetwell Street to West Bars has not yet begun – the old LDEC station must go before that can be accomplished. Dent's old chemist shop has gone (lower right), but the redevelopment opposite the Portland Hotel is still awaiting clearance.

A view from the same vantage point as seen on page 31, taken in 1976. The scene is dominated by the car, with a car park, large traffic island and the Markham Road extension. The Town Hall and Courthouse have replaced Rose Hill and West House respectively, and the AGD will loom large for another twenty-odd years. The Market Hall tower is still without its top.

Chesterfield from the south east, *c.* 1937. Plenty of detail here: at the bottom is the old LMS gasworks and Townrow's Mill. The silk mill on the left is still standing, as are the buildings bounded by Hipper Street, Beetwell Street and Lordsmill Street, and the block to the west of that. The newly erected Cavendish House and Regal cinema stand out top right.

Boythorpe, 1930s. From the south west, showing the new estate, the pattern of the housing seems to leave room for a mirror image to be built on the left in another, future, phase. The tree-lined drive to the right runs through the cemetery, joining Hunloke Avenue at the bottom of the picture. The new William Rhodes School stands out in the middle distance.

Aerial photographs in the early 1920s are rare but this one can be dated by the absence of the Picture House (Odeon) Winding Wheel on Holywell Street, which opened in 1923. Eyres furniture factory on Durrant Road appears darkly to the centre right, and beyond it the GC Station and loop line to Staveley. It may surprise some viewers to see the number of houses in this part of the town, north of Holywell Street, and there were hundreds more just out of the picture.

Lower Brampton in the 1930s. Dominated by the central Robinsons' works, this photograph shows the mostly residential north side of Chatsworth Road and the gas holders, in front of the Goldwell Hill allotments. Plowrights works is on the far left and the Boythorpe Estate lower right.

Pictures from the north are not too common, more detail is usually visible from the south – blame the sun! This view, from around 1938, shows the new Town Hall at the top, and Scarsdale Hospital in the centre, with St Mary's School and the new football ground grandstand on the far right.

The town from the south east in around 1939. Baden-Powell Road curves down from the bottom and, as Park Road, passes Hadfield town next to the Queen's Park. The LDEC platforms can be seen centre right below the new Town Hall. A surprising number of trees, perhaps around the park area, but the pernicious Dutch elm disease would account for the loss of many of these before the end of the century.

The inner relief road, 1995, seen from the church tower, follows the graceful curves of the old LNER railway between roundabouts at the old Horn's Bridge and Whittington Moor. The road, locally nicknamed the 'M½' was opened in 1985, nearly a year ahead of schedule.